Songs *of the* Tongue-Tied

Poetry of the Refugee Experience

FRANCISCO NSABIMANA

Songs of the Tongue-Tied

tellwell

Tellwell Talent
www.tellwell.ca

ISBN
978-0-2288-4712-0 (Paperback)
978-0-2288-4711-3 (eBook)

DEDICATION

Dedicated to Erick Biraronderwa for all the prayers and priceless friendship we had since we were young, my parents for their unwavering support and Mr. Storer for making every dream of mine a reality.

CONTENTS

AUTHOR'S BIOGRAPHY

Francisco Nsabimana was born in Rwanda in 2000. His family was not safe in their home country and fled. Francisco spent his childhood and adolescence in refugee camps in Tanzania, Malawi, and eSwatini. In Malawi, He found his passion in writing from a Writers Club when he was in Dzaleka Community Day Secondary School. He won a scholarship to Waterford Kamhlaba United World College and hopes to continue his education at university in Canada.

Francisco's poems mainly focus on abuse and his experience as a young refugee. The themes running through his poems are suffering, disruption of his education, and gratitude to all who have helped him on the way.

Francisco's poetry is deeply pan-African and is inspired by realities on the continent, from Rwandan history to the HIV epidemic, to pervasive damaging gender norms. His poetry is about his own experiences and those of the people he has met in refugee camps and schools.

Above all, Francisco's poetry speaks of the bonds between people and the compassion and kindness we owe to another. Deeply rooted in the landscapes of sub-Saharan Africa, Francisco's poetry is raw and brutal, while paradoxically brimming with hope.

ACKNOWLEDGEMENTS

Foremost, I would like to extend my heartfelt appreciation to Dr. Selena Rathwell for her continuous support, motivation, and resilience. I would also like to thank her for the immense amount of work she has done in compiling and editing the poems, and in organizing the logistics of this publication. In fact, without her help and support, publishing this book would have remained a nightmarish desire.

Many thanks also to my parents and my siblings for their encouragement and support. Gratitude to Writers' Club at the Dzaleka Community Day Secondary School (DZCDSS) in Malawi, and to all my classmates, friends, and neighbours in refugee camps for their encouragement and motivation. Thank you Biraronderwa Erick and Tuyikeze Elisa for being wonderful and 'bullying' childhood friends and who still are an integral part of my life. Two boys I share the worst and best memories with, much love!

Gratitude to DZCDSS Teachers and staff members in Particular Mr. Kamwani, my Bible Knowledge Teacher and Mr. Gondwe, my Biology, Physics and Chemistry teacher for their love and support when they learned I had some small lines written at the back of my notebooks that were to be called poems. Your support kept me going. My special thanks goes to the family of Erick, in particular Afisa Juma, for being a mother by taking care of our (my siblings and I) needs in the absence of my parents. You are greatly appreciated. To the Jesuit Refugee Service (JRS), a Catholic agency that paid for my school fees in Malawi, and Caritas, who paid for them in Swaziland, thank you. In the absence of their support, publishing this book would have remained a dream.

My sincere and deep gratitude to the United World College community. I extend my thanks to United World College Together for Development Short Course both 2018 and 2019 editions. In particular, I thank Nayantara Mukherji, Joy Dekker and Olga (my umbrella parents), Shakes Dlamini, Nora Uhrig, Lisa Kasamba, Woopi Takarasima and all the facilitators and participants, for your love and encouragement.

To the Waterford Kamhlaba UWCSA (WK) community. Thanks to the teachers and the staff members, especially Sue Bradshaw, my Theory of Knowledge teacher and Extended Essay Supervisor, for caring so much about my story and encouraging me to write. Thanks to Pippa Davies, my English Teacher for reading some of my poems and giving me honest and constructive feedback. Gratitude to Mr. John Storer, Director of Admissions and University Advisor, as your decision has enabled me to write this book. To La familia, Burundian and Rwandan friends in WK who became my family. Your encouragement and support is greatly appreciated. To Mpaka Peers (a community service project started by WK students to help young refugees at Mpaka) your selflessness, resilience and encouragement will always have an imprint on the hearts of young refugees. To Matlala Sefale, (Lesotho, WK 2019-2020) for the photo of the book cover, Anwen Butao, (Malawi, WK 2020-2021) for the Chichewa conversations that triggered some memories I had in Malawi. To Victor Agaba (Uganda, WK 2019-2020) for the encouragement and endorsement of this book, I thank you. Gratitude also to the Advancement Office for including my GoFundMe me campaign in the WK weekly newsletter which undeniably helped raise money for the publication of the book. To Likoebe Maruping, for his generous donation that drove the fundraiser, and to ALL that shared the GoFundMe me link and helped to raise the funds whether directly or indirectly. Thank you to Richard and Josephine Alexander for their support and to Sandra Slind for her editing prowess.

To my writers community, I thank you. To John-Michael Koffi, fellow refugee, UWC student and author of *The Journey Much Desired*, sincere gratitude is due. Without your consultation, this book would never have found its legs. Gratitude also to Lisa Milne, for providing invaluable advice on publishing and the realities of the writing profession. Much gratitude is due to Idowu Omoyele for writing the forward for this book.

Last but not least, I would like to thank all those that either I do not know or have forgotten who fed me, paid my school fees, prayed for me, wished me good luck and still support me. Please receive my heartfelt appreciation.

FOREWORD

Written by Idowu Omoyele (University of Capetown)

Francisco Nsabimana, the Rwandan poet and refugee, is a young man with the potential to develop into one of the outstanding poets of his generation - the cohort of post-Millennials, otherwise dubbed Gen Z, born between the late 1990s and early 2010s. He may indeed go on to create a body of work whose quality transcends the generations. In *Songs of the Tongue-Tied*, his debut collection of poetry, he already shows considerable promise in exploring varied perspectives of the refugee experience in the southern region of Africa. He examines the human condition in lines which hymn odes of love to Rwanda's hilly landscapes and natural streams of flowing water, as well as those which do not flinch from humanity's inhumanity.

The opening couple of poems in Nsabimana's *Songs of the Tongue-Tied* address his native Rwanda with a mixture of ambivalence and pathos. In "Where I Come From", the first poem in the collection, he declares:

> Where I come from,
> Sun lurks on the surface of
> Half-naked children splashing their skin
> Into the chewed bolus of blood
> Where I come from,
> You are woken up by swarms of
> Melodies of the coughing death-stained
> Bolus of blood - where fingers are cast and
> Sprayed onto salt.

In these lines, images of the joyous abandon of scantily clad kids against the lurking backdrop of the sun and those of blood and death commingle. He shows the complexity of 'what is your home. In the second poem appropriately titled "Rwanda", he uses the rhetorical device of apostrophe to directly address, and admit his conflicting emotions about, the country of his birth, a place he is really only able to apprehend or comprehend through books:

> Sometimes I wonder what could have happened
> If the first air I inhaled was not from your trees
> Would I have this courage to stand here
> Or maybe if I had not read about you
> Your love, your tension, both or neither
> It always creates mixed feelings in me Rwanda

And yet, paradoxically, Nsabimana's sense of spiritual distance or estrangement from Rwanda does not preclude him from deriving poetic inspiration from the hills and mountains, rivers and ridges, valleys and and slopes of his native land. These include the hugely important Nyabarongo River, Rwanda's longest river, whose main catchment area is Kigali, Rwanda's capital and largest city; from its source in western Rwanda, it flows towards Kigali, and is a tributary of the Nile:

> The story I wrote with my thin hands
> Wrapped and smeared with soil and reddened heart
> That I collected in a dream beside *Nyabarongo* river
> In the mouth of emptiness
> I learnt that Rwanda is the best, or the prettiest or
> Perhaps the most complicated lesson to
> Comprehend!

In the same poem, he refers to *Nyungwe* and *Akagera* - National Parks in southwestern and eastern Rwanda, sharing borders with Burundi and Tanzania, respectively - and to Mount *Sabyinyo*, an extinct volcano whose peak is intersected by the borders of the Democratic Republic of the Congo, Rwanda and Uganda.

At the root of these complex ties of nationality and kinship lies an historical tragedy which occurred some six years before the birth of Francisco Nsabimana. That is the Rwandan genocide.

Such is the variety of his treatment that his themes range from love for his native Rwanda and gratitude to kind and loving friends, to the scourge of gender-based violence - rape, forced marriage, female genital mutilation - faced by girls and women in, especially, countries in southern Africa; from the HIV/AIDS epidemic, to the legacies of genocide or ethnic cleansing as well as the phenomenon of xenophobia in South Africa; from the stoicism and resilience of widows, orphans and child-headed households, to the hope and distress witnessed in refugee camps, such as the the starvation and malnutrition suffered by displaced peoples as well as the sacrifice and resilience of single mothers.

The speaker of the poem "I Was Sold", written from the perspective of a young woman forced into marriage, ruefully reveals, "When the first clouds gathered to melt the cracks of the earth/ I was sold, I was bought"; she's being sold "to the bellied, ugly and old monster" as wife number seven! The title of the poem "To Whom It May Concern", which deals with rape, also from the victim's point of view, implies that it's being addressed to an anonymous reader or readers, the sort of person or persons so inert or insensitive that they can't be bothered to care about the plight of girls or women whose "pride and dignity" are stolen by their abusers.

In "South Africa's Turning into a Graveyard", the poet indicts the South African xenophobes who shed the blood or cause the death of their fellow black Africans through "the Machete edge's blade", an act of evil lamented even by seagulls; he reminds them of a time, not so long ago, when those fellow black Africans stood with them in the campaign against apartheid:

Do remember when your eyes
Were glued with sorrow, the same
Brothers squeezed and coughed their last blood
Stained cough to smear you ...
So your xenophobic advances
Give them no rest - and feed

Them to your edges and barrel.

The starvation the poet observes while wandering through Dzaleka Refugee Camp is the inspiration for the poem "Sweet". Here, he uses figurative devices like alliteration, anaphora and repetition to talk of "a tree in our orchard" which "produces sweet sweat fruits" which are "their only refresher,/ their only lunch,/ their only dinner,/ Sweet sweat their only sweet sweat for." But fruits, still unripe, are plucked by 'desperate' refugees:

All those around the orchard,
Reap the fruits before the time,
All those on one rope are forced to,
The only reason is hunger.

The corpse of an eleven-year-old girl said to have died of malnutrition, seen by the poet in a refugee camp in 2016, inspires him to ponder death and funerals in "The Grave of Our Being" in which he puns on the word 'grave', as noun and adjective:

The grave is well shaped for our corpses,
The coffin maker is happily chewing himself,
The caution is killing the termites ...
Patiently waiting for our being grave.

Although Nsabimana is not himself an orphan, in "Lenses of My Wishes" he empathizes with those who are, several of whom are his friends; some are in foster care while some are from child-headed households. He admires how they endure their orphanhood with great fortitude and forbearance, how they combine "coiled laughter" with 'choking' with anguish.

"Console My Heart" is inspired by a Congolese widow whom Nsabimana encounters when returning from school; when he asks to help carry her bag, she tells him: "You remind me of my sons who were killed in a war", a remark which leaves an indelible impression on the poet:

Mix my blood with yours,
Wrap my whole with hope,
Perfume my heart to stop nausea,
Give only what is equal to my age.

Do something to wake up my love,
Fuel up my mind to show what I have,
Bandage my heart's wounds,
Teach me what they don't teach in schools.

Water seeds of love in my heart.

Nsabimana's persona or speaking voice displays vulnerability, empathy and humility in addressing a much-suffering Congolese widow whose indomitable spirit he admires, and to whom he makes a plea for warmth, healing, sustenance, wisdom, revival as well as germination of love, strength of mind, protection for a wounded heart. "Console My Heart" is one of the best poems Nsabimana has written.

The title of Francisco Nsabimana's collection of poetry, *Songs of the Tongue-Tied*, is a noun phrase composed of a noun ('songs') and a dependent prepositional phrase ('of the tongue-tied'). The title is ironic, and it is worth considering the keywords in it: 'songs' may refer to melody, tune or vocal music, but poetry, remember, began as song; being 'tongue-tied' denotes inability or disinclination to speak freely or without difficulty, due to shyness, embarrassment, nervousness or surprise. But, as this volume clearly demonstrates, the poet Francisco Nsabimana is anything but tongue-tied. Owing to the intensity and intricacy of his experience, he has a lot to say and does not shy away from doing so.

Idowu Omoyele

December 2020

POEMS

Where I Come From

There is a segment of a thrive,
Caged in a coated stone built in
Its hills, there is a route that
Has cult and bulk in the eyes of its
Frames,
With a continued push to strive and
Survive.

Where I come from,
Sun lurks on the surface of
Half-naked children splashing their skin
Into the chewed bolus of blood
Where I come from,
You are woken up by swarms of
Melodies of the coughing death-stained
Bolus of blood-where fingers are cast and
Sprayed onto salt.

Now, where I come from,
Barrels and edges of whatsoever
Crafts my draft on the sloping
Steps of my ever-weakened desires
A desire blown away by smoke smoked
On its birth age.

Where I come from,
On funeral, we bounce and push over
The anguish on the edge of its tail
"I have lost many".

Where I come from,
New year comes with another anguish
Wrapped in a dark jar, placed on the altar
Hope of grazing the land of their ancestors
Keeps pushing away hope and their wishes in the ambush

Where I come from,
Success is measured by a number of nights
You sleep without walking in your dreams
And days that you taste the rays of the sun with
Both your eyes and throat...

Where I come from,
We have two tongues, one is to glimmer
Glitters and gold about the hidden artefacts
Of the hacked past
The other is to lie- lie about everything-
Our lives, history, future and present.

Rwanda

"Can I tell from the eyes of a protagonist?
No, yes, perhaps both or neither
It pertains with the context of the audience
That's the theory I heard when I was young, Rwanda
It has certainly made me become me.

Sometimes I wonder what could have happened
If the first air I inhaled was not from your trees
Would I have this courage to stand here
Or maybe if I had not read about you
Your love, your tension, both or neither,
It always creates mixed feelings in me Rwanda

Slowly I grew to understand that whoever spoke evil
About you unconsciously pushed meditation into my mind,
I am attached to you, yes I can feel you in my veins.
I read both your stories, your opinions, your tragedies,
Your opinions and your elegance.
Yet nothing moves me, my heart remains fixed.
Let me tell a story!

ONCE UPON A TIME
There lived a mother, her name was Rwanda, had power over everything,
Heaven and hell, in fact both.... But many preferred hell over heaven
Blood over milk
But this mother hated both, either or neither
It was never clear to her
One day a passenger passed by and found two sons and asked
Them if peace would be over pieces…
Blood over milk...
Hell over heaven...
All chose peace, blood and heaven.... Why blood?
Here is the story!!!

The story I wrote with my thin hands
Wrapped and smeared with soil and reddened heart
That I collected in a dream beside *Nyabarongo* river
In the mouth of emptiness
I learnt that Rwanda is the best, or the prettiest or
Perhaps the most complicated lesson to
Comprehend!
Your name Rwanda takes away my
Nameless pain which pursued my sorrow
Wrapped about my life......
You have been my role model... Yes
The moderator of my thoughts

My father before he grew lines on his forehead
Told me to never push you ahead or before my heart
You should always dance, dine and deliberate with me
That you never cease to feed the eyes of the seeker
And spectator with your evergreen and ever clean
Walled and streamlined thoughts and streets
Landscapes and your thousands of hills.
From the young age he told me to always look into your eyes
And do what you signal me to do
To look at your dressing code and dress like you
To read about you!
To talk like you
And sleep like you.......
But that I should choose peace over milk
For the well sleeping snores to maintain
Its tunes and for the awake souls to feed
And sip on!

He said my ears will never go deaf
From your sons *Intore*
Dancing with their softer bones
And melodies being overtuned
On the retrieved and slapped shakes of the wind.

Your river reminisces Rwanda
The beauty of your thin-wrapped forehead
And *Nyungwe* whose heart beats bursts with
Swollen desires of elegance
Chance and menace of this race paces
Awes of those whose pockets swells with
Money and eyes longing to see your beauty beyond trace......

Proudly tell them of your *Akagera* and *Sabyinyo*
The only shade that shades shattered- hearts from shelter
Of shame and shocks, shocked by shocks of sharks
Oh! Rwanda, only if once upon a time, could remain once upon a time.

Road

You that never ends,
Your names fantasize me
You that never shakes off one's sleep
Your thorny path sets ablaze my melody,
I talk of you road that scorches my throat

You that never sleeps, but snores in my mind
I am done rehearsing your coiled brutality!
You that never smells, but sniffs like an endangered dog
I am to you and you to me
Now in the battle

You, yes, I talk of you that escalates
The rain in the flooding streams,
You that dries up the tears of mourning widows
You that shakes hands with both hands and shock
Hearts only with thoughts,
Mine thoughts have decided to weed you out

You that never lets the share of the heart dance,
Who never gives the wind a plain chance
You who blows the gums of teeth in tails of the mouth
You the road that stretches
The forgotten reminiscence.

Crippled Mind

My mind proposed hope,
My soul brewed relinquishment,
The rain brew on the top,
My heart needed quenching.

Feigned words lazily relaxed,
Jerusalem city immersed in blood,
Jeremiahs were highly perplexed,
Tedious and laborious tears, bald.

The mind of him oozed out,
The strength of his became salty,
It was his life or his death,
The fogging hand got amputated.

"Sorry, Sir for selling your sad soul!"
A trembled tale taunted through his tears,
Though this truth was taught,
Mark if his mind was muted madly,
The crippled mind, the crippled life.

Lenses of My Wishes

The books of quietness and calmness
Wired in cemented roads,
Chuckles of coiled laughter and
Mixed choking well,
Lenses of my wishes brightened
Colourful with a flourishing dance
A carnival of my nights in a health
Tombs of a chance.

Lenses of my wishes, trimmed on
The top of a four-legged kettle on
The crossed-palm of the dusty road,
Whitened on a sharp-edged pump
Pump of the wetted smell of
Exhausted blood,
Of a jump of the humping jungle
In a wavering camp...

Cut-open woods, sliced into bunches
Of a fast-fading voice of my wishes,
Tortured, and splayed on the
Covered layer of its lenses...
Die, or be born into a mortal
Creature, which breeds with its wishes.

Sweet

There is a tree in our orchard,
The tree produces sweet sweat fruits,
They are usually plugged immature,
The only reason is desperate.

All those around the orchard,
Reap the fruits before the time,
All those on one rope are forced to,
The only reason is hunger.

Food without fruit sweet sweat,
Forbidden is anything without sweet sweat
The reason why is 'we are grown here'

Their only refresher,
Their only lunch,
Their only dinner,
Sweet sweat their only sweet sweat for.

South Africa is Turning Into a Graveyard

Choke the vessel, unbound to its
Ways, stroke t-t-t-t-t blood- lurking,
On the Machete edge's blade,
Ever seen this lethal death, squashed
Shshsh…plays? Unbalances the
Shield of the shade-

Waves and flies of toxic leaflets
Populated on the throats of the East,
Calmed voices of tyrant groans
Geared on the spark of her roots,
Your forehead same coated in-
Melanin, likened to a beast-
Walking-query slowly cascades
The waiting clouds from its books

The seagulls, everywhere laments
Darkens the future as long as your
Passport shows another chamber
Of your house, your consanguinity
SA your blood… your cement
Branched grass of boiled hons to ensnare
Your voices.

Those that shone in the middle
Of their nightmares, brushes their
Teeth with sand…gasoline lurks,
And stops their pulse…
Death lingers and snatches their
All aspired chase-desired base

SA turns into graveyard,
Wooded in the buttons of bruised
Loathe concocted in the darkest
Beam, clasped in the mean
Of shocking off dust, tilting down
The so-long cut yard-it relents,
Seduces earthquake, and reconnects
The long-deserted dream.

Do remember when your eyes
Were glued with sorrow, the same
Brothers squeezed and coughed their last blood
Stained cough to smear you…
So your xenophobic advances
Gives them no rest-and feeds
Them to your edges and barrel.

Console My Heart

Mix my blood with yours,
Wrap my whole with hope,
Perfume my heart to stop nausea,
Give only what is equal to my age.

Do something to wake up my love,
Fuel up my mind to show what I have,
Bandage my heart's wounds,
Teach me what they don't teach in schools.

Water seeds of love in my heart.

The Grave of Our Being

The house is long and magnificent,
The road is too thin and thorny,
The house's door is too dark,
The grave of our being is already ready,
The miles we walk with sweat in us,
Obligations turned against us completely,
The grave of our being is really,

The grave is well shaped for our corpses,
The coffin maker is happily chewing himself,
The caution is killing the termites...
Patiently waiting for our being grave.

Life isn't really straight,
The Angels of it aren't equal for real,
The life's melting point has melted,
The grave of our being is too resistive.

Dig Harder, it is Down

We are given blunt knives to dig,
We chew the jobs with gladness,
With all our little collected strength,
We are frowned upon blamed for everything,
"...dig it harder it is down…"

Thirst encroaches our throats happily,
The hunger becomes our permanent visitor,
The poorest education, health assimilate us,
The only enslaver is murmurings of owners,
"...we dig it harder probably it is down..."

Dying slowly, happily is at its peak,
Our systems are no longer at their positions,
Even our tears only left strong are weak,
The environment predators force illusion.
".... To dig it harder down…"

We at night warm ourselves with cold,
We eat our lunch at graves mourning,
We too drink and clothe insults...
"...Then malnutrition digs our brothers harder..."

Lies

Once you can walk on the clouds
And play a *Kinyarwanda* song
Interwoven with a dream
You will sing in blue seas.
These are not lies

The view of your lies
Lies in the steepest eye
In the clearest wind
Afloat
Across
The lies of a century

Lies slaying down a muddy street
Lies that birds sing in unison
Tied and wrapped on her neck
Overflowing in the current of her days, the thoughts...

You see, lies that hide beneath thousand
Heaps of truth of forbidden remedy
Forbidden explanation
Captured and thrown in *Kivu*
Overflowing the current of
Her wishes, her desires

Maman Africa

Haunting chastity of slavery that tasted your feet,
Roams the icons of my mind.
Your sons and daughters that are engulfed by sharks
In crossing Mediterranean,
Distorts my breathing patterns.
The silenced screams of your daughters
Being sexually mutilated,
Boils my anger and forces smoke out of my nostrils.
Oh! Maman, your eyes are reddened like lips
Smeared by lipstick.

Skulls and bones of your children crushed and broken in
Rwandan genocide, thwarts my forehead.
Your daughters that Bokoharam has disgraced by undressing
Their dignity, their façade resemblance touches my feet.

The feud that your own children showed during xenophobia
In South Africa,
Melts my melting solubility.
Your daughter Somalia, whose hands and feet
Are still dissolved in blood,
Expostulates my neurons' speed.
The detrimental cyclone idai that stretched itself
On bed of your triplets Mozambique, Malawi and Zimbabwe, shakes
My tenderness and honest consensus with anger. Oh maman!

Your south Sudanese and Somalians
Children rotting and being fed to vultures of insurmountable
Hunger In the refugee camps, disturbs the route of my consciousness.
Your atmosphere that brews anger, hatred and hazardous gases,
Dries up my throat.

Maman Africa
Your heart has grown fonder,
And history has left all the pages
Plain with the darkest cloud,
This torments my aspirations.
Look at your prettiest daughter DRC being spat on
After being pillaged, raped and monopolised,
This compels the compass of my eyes to UN.
Oh maman... Am sorry,
Your way of healing has been framed as witchcraft,
And your herbs burnt, a long forgotten heritage,
You have been left naked.
This burst bruises loneliness in my soul.
The ropes and chains tied on your neck and wrists,
Drags my years long miles like the Nile river.

And the wounds that miles imposed
On your legs and head, races my costumes
And threatens my harmony.
Countless daughters and some that Scourge, AIDS
Has snatched from you,
Replayed are their souls on your forehead....
Africa, I sob, but in the loudest silence.

If Death Could Wait

Let me tell you a story
If death could have waited
I would have tapped my dreams in
The light-struck thunderstorm.
Only if the machete never hacked my neck!

If I didn't die the way I did
I would have clung to the itching and
Comforting hymns of the sermon,
I would have raised my children
I would have fed them to crawling wind

If death could wait,
I would only need a razor and a book,
A razor to sharpen my growing teeth,
A book to travel far from the world
Into the furthest brains of knits...
If only it could wait...

If dying had a stop,
I would have waited for arrival centuries ago,
Till a heart of life of hopes
Dies, fades and waves
Only if death could wait

If crying had reddened my thoughts,
And prolonged captions of wishes,
Facets of the green graves would have
Sunken my intuition,
And shake my ablutions-
With its casted cross on the
Doorway of the catapulted wishes…
If only that oxygen had lingered more…

Subordinate clause of my shocked doze, acclimatized
The roots of my anchor-
Quenched dry throat of my days
With bluffed quake and dipped quest
Of my life…

If only death had waited, I would drill a sharp.

At Least Spare None

At least kill only the dying soul
And save the blossoming slumber
Body,
For the dying fades into air
And mitigate eternity
And blossoming sprouts broken
Hopes, emerging desires.

But if you assault both, leave no trace
Leave only what is lifeless and defenceless,
And if you spare, spread venom
And dry the cells on the whirling fire
Oh! No, on shaking tender

Leave no soul to exhume my
Long-coveted wish
Petals are slacking and ripening,
Fresh buds shall arise,
But only if these branded branches
Are terminated, no, when they
Are relieved
At least spare none.

You see, when I woke up, my father...
All what good life requires,
And all that ringing and thrilling
Wealth sang collaboratively in choirs
My legs if moved 50 metres further and now

Shade has smoked my
Life,
Wealth and health all has been dimmed
Together, with my fastened day,
Imagine, the following day, I was
Millions of metres away from home,
From paradise,
I felt if hell existed,
Then I should be its mask it for my tongue
To at least taste a liquid, red-liquid, blood
Not anymore, I locked my soul in the tree leaves
And tied my hunger and tears on the
Pass on way of *Nyungwe*

Peace

Should I compare you to the attainment of a feeling?
distraught, with a zipped heart or caged syllable in the den of fear?
Or cancer that unwinds my curved cells?
Or the mine that never gets extracted?

Like smoke, you colour the cells of the holiness of unholy, they misuse.
Should I compare you to silence?
Because the silenced, mistakes have gotten you, and those with peace do mistake to have been silenced.

You are bizarre!
You crave your way through everything, everywhere and nowhere at all.

Remember when I was a toddler your whispers, zzz only could be heard six million years back in time...groans, hopelessness, hunger, or maybe or those that are supposed to come with you, never crossed my eyes!

Only birds sang that hope, and half- naked toddlers sang in unison, in your smoke, in your shadow!

Unhealed Wound

My sunlight how did dark come,
I lived because of your only light,
My moonlight how did the fate tame,
I now live only on a torn apart lite.

I tired my legs in fruitless forests,
When now asked about my wound,
It's worse, worse and worse rotten,
The roaring war followed my footsteps.

I tried clinics, hospitals even witchdoctors,
With great nausea, they found out origin,
Sent back my neurons to mouth of sharks,
And then piled up their documents and depart.

My unhealed wound still stinks, isolated,
It is isolated, isolated by its originality,
It has professional but negligence,
My unhealed, oh! My wound when...

Life in a Closed Camp

She asked when she saw lamenting children,
"...the mouth of the shark..."
They fast against their will
Their bleeding eyes choke them to death.

She had a chance to converse with success,
"...I won't grant them status...
They are species of war not of success
I will only give them a chance to chase".

She asked hunger why it torments them
"...they have no access to food source ....
They are neglected I hug them with happiness
To eradicate me it needs only well- wishers".

She had a chance to meet Mr. Hope,
"... Only the background was stolen, not future...
Their tears are wiped only by me,
Success is my brother, they will have him".

Steady Mountain

I met lonely souls in the camp,
Discussing their loneliness to their mates,
Their originality ignores their personality,
The nakedness of being a refugee torments their mentality.

I had this and that,
Now only left with finger nails to scratch myself,
My life's pursuit barren can't hatch,
My mind and mouth dehydrated.

She alone standing in scorching sun,
She alone talking to her soul alone,
She alone as an island troubled alone,
Heaviness of history steals away her happiness.

Given cheque to madness against her will,
Removed in the clique of healthier people,
Her consanguinity still unfulfilled as a parent,
Has a lot to show to her children,
Nature taking charge on her breathing pattern,
The sender and commander of mercy, show her one!

I Was Sold

You see that cow, the fattest one?
It makes me vomit, chokes me

Its belly grew from my virginity
Its milk is the last drop of blood from my lungs.

Covered by the cloud of the night
Zoomed cars and mouths negotiated my price

Stunned were their eyes, skipping the dusty
Insects rebuilding on their foreheads.

I was to be sold, to the bellied, ugly and old monster
and became a Savior of my family

Munyana cried
She was younger, and the same wind would whirl her soon

When the first clouds gathered to melt the cracks of the earth
I was sold, I was bought

When he came with *Urwarwa* and
Inka, my parents danced songs in their ears
Here is the man.
That I would be the seventh didn't matter to them
As long as their hands stopped itching
And their thoughts got smoothen by *urwarwa* and milk of the fattest cow

Ten years died, and ten children came
Hot splashes of days kept me darker
Every fruit had the same height
Their bones easily registered on their frail bodies, frail spirits
Frail souls.

Mine Belief

Red petals that wilted the melting sun
Stigma that sounded less than bees along
A day, casted with shun
Retrieves and reveres leaves of a long time
That's not mine belief

Mine belief that no hand can't
Stretch for the cliff of hope
That every word can travel on
The miles of ones aspirations
And desires
Mine belief, that salt smelted in one's mouth
Restores honour and dignity.

Sunlight and moonlight of my
Nestled hopeful cries and mornings
Slept aspirations and showcased
Heart and mind desires... To
Revere peace of dignity.
That's mine belief

The only belief that no
Look, height, walk or dreams travel
On vegetal mind's stimulations
like love.

When I Cried

When I devoured dusty-mud-
Polished with a pulse of bliss
You waved a reckoning card
Amounting to a massed kiss
When I cried, your pulse
Inflated and conflated.

When years wore on, conjectures
Rerun all over my confined shade
Delineated my head when away
For my food adventure,
Tumped together, I was as sharp as blade
But only when I cried
That concocted the shaky tender dried in my eyes.
Whenever turbines of my deeds
Overturned its current,
Like a soothing wave, you stormed into
The swans and dispersed
The seeds,
And diverge my diverged tent.

When, sometimes I overstate your
Presence in mine life,
I cry and sob with both my
Heart and soul,
When all you did recollect and recoil
To push me from plight,
Forces my life from Saul to Paul...

It is the day, when the cloud
Recanted on the edge of its arisen
Around joy,
When the creature to push the bottom
Breathed the air, but when I cried
You cried as well and wrapped me in
Your worn hands and prayed.
I will never forget
Or forget when I cried

Before I Die

When all I dreamt of will cease,
And all the steps recoil slowly,
I want my inner shift to race the races before I die.

Before I die,
I want to have been there,
As a rescue of floating dreams,
And cease the ceaseless.

I want my voice to be hoarse,
Before I die,
Talkative and encroached to inaugurate
A voice to the voiceless,
To tap the times and melodies,
To the ears of those days on the edge of death,
To smoothen the chewing,
And cunning that enslaves those at birth,
I want to be of that use before I die.

I want my slavery to be somebody's gains before I die,
My sweat to molest monsters,
Of poverty of others,
My hand to dive lengthy paths,
In all the pastures,
Yes, I want all that before I close my eyes forever.

All I desire before I descend six feet down,
Is to design a forest that never wilts,
A sky that is generous enough,
A day which knows no displacement,

Before my pages get stripped of dignity,
I wish to reconcile the author
And the pages,
Before I decide to shift my life to heaven,
Where I shall cross my fingers
And sip on heaven's milk,
I want to at least hike one's life
Before I die.

Dreams

Harness the dwindled thorny path, cast on the edge of the shadow,
Hanged on the zeal of passion are my desired dreams,
Those that I have dreamt with a heart that is hollow,
And burnt its choking essence on the brewing rocketed streams.
My dreams, my strings that I have held under my armpits, and have tainted my gone mind flips.

Whenever, I dream, I walk in mine dreams,
Don't ask me how, but I have tasted this desire,
Desire to dream and bream at the same time...
Dreams that have been battened on the waves of change but remain uncovered.
Dreams that I have scattered on the bank of Tanganyika and have been shipped to the future
My dreams, my fantasies.

Those dreams that I had, tapped between my teeth, scorched my face and tilted my forehead with a beam of capsized trails.
Though it has happened, it has also remained a dream, a dream that is as intangible as Serengeti Park, loaded with leaned running waters.
My dreams have shriveled and dispelled my latter on the shore of its tails.

To Whom it May Concern

Whoever it may concern, let it be your concern.
That they are millions am certain
Their pride and dignity taken
Health and wealth are mistaken
Let it be read by birds and boiling days
Where no actor is different from shutter

To whom it may concern,
Thatched tent lying on my hairy chest
Dried in the creamed hatred...
Pointed on my nose...and reddened by my light
When it may spark interest into,
Re-equate bleeding smell of my hallucinations
Prostates calamity in my ears...

To whoever it may concern in the oval-shaped mountain
Fountain of my stained turn and burn
Whoever this fading melodies- channels this to;
Dive, cry and dry its smoke and disperse it to the inhabited grounds.

Where I Kept My Soul

Where stars shine to the shore,
Where failure has no cult,
Where septic and vagued songs are sung,
Where a take gives a take and a give gives a take,
I covered my soul in it.

On a spring board where bold hates cold,
I boarded a boat bought from abroad,
Heading to the breeze breaths which bonded,
And was a bond to my soul,
This is where I laid my soul.

In a tank full of a mixture of various substances,
Is where I trusted, rested and immersed my soul
In a plumbed, roughed and unsteady steep slope,
Subsided and subdued site is the side I sat,
Slept and soothed my soul.

In thick rains where no sound of hate was heard,
Where moons summon to chitchat with sun,
Is where I threw my soul, where only the flag,
Of cowardice is flogged, folded and forbade and,
Where when what whose what was seen where?
Is where I kept my soul.

You Are My Desert

The dance you danced last time,
The brewing and choking look you looked at me last time,
The share your heart beat shared with me,
Cut off my spine!

The gaze that stormed into my eyes,
The movement that shook off my tenderness,
The glory you stripped me off,
Still haunts my days and nights,

You see that you grew taller than your height,
You overtook your own sense of reasoning,
You invited the devil with your own hands,
You beckoned trouble by your own look and fragrances!

You see that I am crying in a suffocating firewood smoke,
My bush is burning,
I am deserted!
Look my eyes have grown red,
My heart is darkened!
You have added charcoal to my heart!

The pit we dug together got filled,
The boat we drove wrecked,
And the paths we crossed got thorny,
You planted the thorns, didn't you!!?

You see that whenever I dream I shout,
It's because I slept with the buzzing horns,
Do you see that whenever I call your name obstinately holds my throat,
It's because I forgot to close that door of elongation, I wish I had closed!

Don't worry, you are my water's heat,
You are the storm and flood in my thoughts, you are my desert!

Her

A day that cast darkness,
Chemicalised and liquefied day,
Less were the visual of the days,
The day that was engulfed by raised eyelids,
The day that rain sprew and splashed the poet's melting hand,
The purification of the day that ceased ceaselessly.

Her, a joke that splitted my lungs,
Sped up and filled the cup of agony,
Lazily and restlessly tortured my veins,
A joke that restricted my inner monsters,
Suspicion that catapulted empty interest,
A joke that choked my day...

Her, a riddle that no one knows of,
Regardless of how hard I tried,
Whose meaning deflects the heart- beat,
Whose explanation needs a speared mind aside,
A riddle that creates periods,
A riddle that will never quench my relentless curiosity.

Her, a flower that has no stigma,
That dry and cracked weather....
Visits less,
A multicolored flower, with choking scent and frankincense,
A flower, whose roots cut....
A flower which captivates eyes for eternity...

Her, the brain that is vaccinated,
The brain whose nerves are not electrical,
Whose apprehension bentds... at right angle,
A brain that cares less about passing breezes,
A brain worth taking a bullet for,
A brain that has no holes....

Her, a heart that never faints,
Whose ways are rational and dilated,
A heart that shakes shakely the reshaped thoughts,
The heart that hates hurting...
The heart that no one knows of...... But exists.

Only I

The scent of soft splashes of rain, fantasizes me
When it heals the cracked land,
It caresses my nostrils
When deserted grounds taste the lurking hill of water
This chemistry lures me.

The north and south moves of my body
The dancing tone countered
With blossoming body, thwarts my head
The medicine to my hardened spell of trouble
Ohh my God! Dancing
The only stabilising table

I can't throw away my music desires afloat
Ever seen him, the handsomest, the best Burna,
Ever seen his moustache?
Ever got sipped on his trembling voice?
Ever seen his body? The sexiest!
It's covered in the frankincense of Jerusalem
Like a tiger complacent on its prey
Walahi! Nitasahawu kusali!

Ever seen my curved body in skirts?
Ever seen my shaped shape?
It scares me! How do you see it?
Or should I say the meeting of my creation was the longest?
It's elegant, soaked in blades of beauty, perhaps of
Ulembo!

Ever seen my breasts sniffing in my chest?
Embroiled with my hoodie?
Ever overheard my breasts conversation?
Eeee bwana, the perfect size
Or perhaps the worst of the best!

I should confess before going!
Tunes, well-knitted melodies,
Cast stars,
Rolling of auto-tuned tempo
Haki ya mungu, fantasises me,
And disturbs my thinking!

Come and See

Take away my heart and leave my eyes,
To roll itself on those slippery slope of colours
Dazzling looks of petals
Have you seen it glittering?

Ever swallowed and chewed music?
I do!!
When its echoes fly on the kit of waves and
React with my ears,
My brain creeps, and my body becomes defenceless
Then nod the head
Then my frail hand
Then follows the obstinate dance
The moves of the don't moves me

Ever seen me in gumboots?
Of course not!
I am a cook of dreams!
A server of happiness!
A diver of diving stars!
An eagle on a basketball....
When sweat nuances my forehead!
Packed with oversized shorts!
Complimenting colours!
My hair curled together!
My back rests only in the box!
Any argument?

Do bury your head in your lap
And loneliness not solitude kisses your mind,
And let your ears stretch
And let the nails of your dreams be driven
By the current of waterfalls
Current of frequencies of the heart,
Amplitudes of the brain,
Deserts of the desires!

I was advised not to look at her
But that's not my design
Her dances, her songs, her everything
"Diamonds" that has been a stain, stained on the walls
Of my heart
On the firewall of my brain!
Though I try I fail, I should be prodigal on this one!

And that can't define me!
Enough, like the choking smell
That soothes my airways,
Smoothens my splendour
Ohhh! That's the smallest snippet of my story!

Hold Those Knives in My Heart

With vigour and laughter
Slice my heart and sprinkle in it salt
Let the current take them into my veins
On my suitcases and my tiptop chains

Like a rolling stone,
Drive me down the shore
Where my heart shall taste the taste of my unconscious
Dreams and cemented sleep slopes of Nyabarongo
And the shaking tendons of flattened roads of Rwanda

Hold at a hand that squeezed love
And press it deep into my chest,
My nest, where my haste hatches
And tilt my eyebrows with that
Memories childhood touch from
Mbonimpa and and Bimenyimana
In looking for doors of water
In the deserted desert, dejected
Feelings

Hold those knives in my heart
In time when the sun tastes and casts
The sharp blades of the sun
Let the knives shrink my vessels
Build that thorned fence
Alone gone, and forever lost
In the mountains of loneliness
I want the shielding of your knives
In mine heart's memories

Let that dip-drop into my casted wind
Wind from the *Akanyaru* river
With my cursed and loathed loved-
And let those knives take apart my current
My torment sharp standing statues of stairs
Of knives in my heart... In my future
Hold these knives in my heart.

Sit Down My Son

Whenever you cross paths of needy,
And your pocket is swollen,
Don't bite your hand,
Personify your hand to be a hook,
And book a sip for the needy,

Sit down my son, raise your ears.
Whenever you raise the heat of emotions,
Don't stand tall on your 'manhood'
Let your knees taste the ground
And let mucus smoothen your throat
Your voice box push forward the sweetest
Remorseful melody,
And apologize without seeing the
Meters of the response of dignity.

And my son, if you marry and
Find your wife not a virgin,
Don't let that poison your marriage
I married your mother millions years ago
When marriage was arranged
When our feet knew no shoes,
When we met under a tree
Not beaches, at dusk and on wells not in cinemas,
Times change my son, respect that.

Whenever, a pen favours your desires,
Don't force forget it up in into your head,
Don't abuse the air and molest
The lungs it passes through
Take half the result of your ink
And paint it with the dying...
My son, listen to my word...

And whenever you fall in love...
Know culture, height, history has
No blood relation with love…
This strongest accent of the world
Will lose your heart
And whenever heavy words slip into
Your love,
Let it fade into the air like dew
Once it encounters the day
Let it jump out
Don't corner it
My son, sit down and listen to me…

When you wake up, don't forget to pray
Seize the chance and loiter
The monsters of evil
When your friend calls in need
Like wind to the smoke, rise
And visit him
For what knocked on his door
Lingers around still...
Don't let this run away from your heart.

My son, it was long ago when
Boys were considered better than
Girls.
I regret to have educated you
And neglected your sister.
Be the driver and introduction
To uplifting them,

My son, don't be thorns in others'
Wounds,
My son, be a stretched hand
To everyone
My son, sit down, before I sleep.

Your Death

Your death, father,
Fed me to a monster with sharp-claws
Anguish, anger, essence of death
Corroded in my thick ears,
My long-deserted worry, resurrected
Choked my thoughts and strangled my voice,
Your death, father left me scattered on the dry
And cracked smiles…

Your death, mother,
Darkened the shadow of my life
And married me to torture and silence
Neared me to overturning turbines of
Salty seas…
Pushed smoke of solitude into my nostrils
Pushed me into the flames of fire.
Your death, mother orphaned me
Twice, and threw me into thorns

Your death, virginity,
Fed me to threats of suicide
When his arduous smell cut you open
You screamed and your screams faded into
Thick air,
You had waited nearly for two decades
You had tasted both the tenders
And had hidden yourself in the shades
And then came shutters and pillagers
Your death virginity, blame it on
Your uncle, who tamed you in the ashes…

Your death, love,
Was precipitated by your uncle
When he sneaked into your room
Squeezed opium into your drink
And amputated you, and left you
Bleeding,
Cut you with sharp razor blades
Castrated and eradicated you…
The waves of your heartbeat, the
Flaws and eloquence
The turbines, the feud, was molded
Your death love, left me a scar
Unhealing wound
Strong essence of hatred.

Your death, body,
Came when your uncle showered me with sickness.
It's not funny, don't laugh
Neither is it entertaining,
His oversized organ, fed me cancer,
His unzipped zip, molested my immune
You died, and I cremated you
I hardly get better, I hardly chew
Any word or thoughts
Your death, body, brought the death
Of your wishes.

Your death, hope,
Pushed memories on the back of my neck
Recycled my days and poured me to its edge
And reaped all the ingrained-sways of light from my arms.

Only My Heart

When I died, I saved you in my surface
I sent my feelings to the eternity
To clean up my chopped mess
I could extend my love to the infinity,
Even though I died, only my heart kept beating....

When I fasted for a century, without a leak licking my
Burning throat,
I drowned in the solitude or
Perhaps the forbidden swans of sentiments,
When my heart plotted conspiracies to
Cut my throat,
I claimed to have warned my inner desires as its presents
Only my heart, ruled, and guided

When I decided to print an ounce of an
Ink in my plain, deserted pages of love
It dawned, and remained unknown for decades
With only my heart, flattened like flapped wings of a dove
Pain shook my brains
To multitudes of anguish...
Only my heart remained innocent and deserted...

When we met in dreams, I asked
If you could stay much longer, but you said
Your heart was in million streams
In the shadow of penumbras
And stretched only my heart longer...
It was a confession of a century......
Only my heart woke me up, warmed me and alarmed me.

When our eyes were to be blocked by distance
I sent a wave of a deadly wish
A wish for you to remain in my dreams, in my memory
To confirm to that I was being covered with hot ashes,
You threw me to the longest strain, stance, solace...
Only my heart suffered
Or maybe stiffened!

In Those Days

Ha! No one knew the stretch would be stretched,
No one dreamt of being crowned the princess of epitome,
No one had her date inscribed on the bed of the lovely mother's fate,
It just happened and alarmed everyone.

In those days, legs talked,
Mouths walked,
And voices dreamt and moulded,
There was no reality or possibility of anything,
Not even an air!
In those days, her life had no campus!

She slept with her wishes and aspirations,
She was great in bed,
She delivered a healthy and peaceful baby
She had no breasts to nurse it, she had to let it go,
No! She didn't!
She carried and nursed it, till it grew,
We are the by-products of this sweat!

In those days, when even a drop of blood would quench millions' thirst,
In those days one's life span equated to the setting sun, there was no roof to it.

In those days streets were there, but unnamed,
Rivers were there with another colour!
Of course even greediness existed, but with an honorable name.
And love did but soaked in a bitter solution.

Untold Heroine

Sometimes a day comes in haste,
Sometimes one's dream is wasted,
And sometimes one's eye does the taste,
And one's name leaks to the dreaded!

I have tightened my belt,
Nothing I don't do, I am a parent,
The fruits, that my blown away spouse gave me,
Like cracked ground in Sahara, salivate my sweat,
And miles 'toujours' tastes my dilapidated feet,
And my eyes graduated from tears ages ago!

There are not just children I care,
But frail, body malnourished by hunger,
Haunted mind traumatized by the best monster,
Which was trained by best,
Hands that slept on the trigger that best in choking one's mind and life with,
Floods of emptiness and hopelessness!

It's always hard to tell her not to follow men,
When the love of the father never crossed her paths,
When she menstruated once in three months,
Due to anemia,
When she relied on her only 'gifted' body,
To pave her fasted way to grave to peace,
Out of the torture of her mind.

Guide me! How can I tell James to stop drugs,
When it's only where he finds refuge,
And how can I ever call myself a mother,
When blood is polluted by venom,
Genocide still threatens the mind,
Of my fruits, my children, my hope!

I last tasted smiles when in my country,
Of origin, drifted and dragged into slippery water,
Meat, or fashions never dares nears itself to,
My mind, my swollen brain will
Suffocate it

Freed From Hostage

When a soul dies before the body
The bruises of the heart float,
When cries and groans reloads the load,
Death capsizes boats.

Where are the people?
Dark-sea waters lamented loudly,
"Here, we are" they were three people
Shook tender from their teeth...
And went on errands into the dark forests...

Oiled the dog wounds of the soul,
Loosened the strings of solitude
Whispered a wave of a change
And chained me free from solitude...
Cut pieces of my groans,
And replayed memories of an urge...

Their blood dear,
Are red stained with a willing heart,
Their feet dear,
Were enslaved by sores of benevolence
Their soul dear, others hearts
Kept awake to shake dust off
Their prayers dear,
Are directly channeled to the
Listener to the ears of the high ranked.

I had dreams,
Dreams that were very uncertain,
But stars came and shook me, and guided me.

Much can't be done
Words can't skin your stiffened
Heart of glory,
May an ink, ink the right,
Hand be stretched free from tire
And strings of your brains be loosened.

United World

A mother to orphaned hopes
Hopes which are dry
Hopes which hold no water to others,
Hopes, yes aspirations
She nurtures and waters
And freely let them flow to the world.

A family that is a bazaar
Whose genetics nobody understands,
Biracial, blacks, whites, Indians, Asians
All are its favourable daughters and sons
Has homes in east, west, south, north
The family which is everywhere.

A movement that drafts the move
The movement of its thighs,
Nobody imitates
The kindness elegance she wears on her neck
Unique helping curve that no one has,
Eyes that see beyond oceans of future
And a heart that pumps greatness to the world.

Rain that wets inhumane hopes
And slides through its veins and brains
And chains its ways away...
A table where hunger never dares stretch itself
A house whose windows and doors
Knows no closure
A book whose authors' brains are soaked in peace
And a bridge whose walls never trembles.

If I Would Create

If my hands had formulas of beauty,
If my shoulders rubbed powder of calamine,
If my eyes were shiny like yours,
Then I would create you a twin, a congruent figure
For the world would be blessed to have many of you.

If I would thank the smoulder of your soul,
Then the universe would know it,
He left nothing untied,
You are a true fresh bunch to the tree,
And that the same day your parents were blessed with a gift of a baby girl,
A changer.

Your name, there was not any taste of underestimation in that,
Your parents completely meant their words....
You whose nose and fingers, politicize the fasting souls of many,
You whose brain never sleeps without dreaming of shifting and stretching others,
You whose age has no ounce of relation to your capability,
Ohhh my God,
If I would create, you would go far, where no selfish look would shook or hook me, and nkigana imana,
I would definitely christen my thoughts your name,

I would mould a cloak that would symbolize that Jesus slept into when he was born,
I would surpass and adjust the love that you show to your friends,

And if I would create, I would imitate your intelligence and bear my own child the same date as you were born,
The day that God spat air into the universe,
The day that darkness broke up with light, and,
Never returned,
The day that smelled of fragrances.

Oh my God if only I was at least half of you,
I would create a table that knows no turning that would feed your soul and continue watering you,
And that, this is a new year to you,
And that you have crossed over.

If only I would create.
I would transform all people into you.

Thank You Mom

Oh! Failure don't you feel uncomfortable
In the presence of this success?
Don't you feel suffocated by the fragrant smell from her nose?
Can't you recognize you no longer have freedom and opt for the suicide?
This success is you mom, Asante.

Oh! Hunger do your roots ever get water again to blossom you?
With this heart filled with granaries of food.
Don't you feel useless and naked once you find yourself homeless?
Can't you see rain and sun is now in equilibrium; you are now an outcast!
This heart is you mom.

Oh! Night, do you think we are no longer afraid of your sharp blades?
No, not in the presence of this brightest torch!
Don't you believe with the view that we are nor moved an inch by your approach?
Can't you see our arms are heavily loaded with an everlasting torch!
This torch is you, mom, Zikomo.

Oh! tribulations, do you ever call yourself a threat again? With this Moses in our midst?
Don't you ever get teased with the ten plagues?
Can't you see your threats are harmless and that our minds are free?
This Moses is you, mom, Murakoze.

I Am a Poem

I am a light illuminating in the dark
A day enclosed in the darkest and brightest light,
A horse running flapping its tail
A fish suffocated with oxygenated water,
I am a poem.
Which flows no path of any
Which flows flawlessly,
Which chokes less disastrously
And which gathers no discouragement.

I am a tree planted in a rocky rock
A mirror which gives no reflection,
A rumour which is spread by nobody
A song which nobody wills to sing,
And a dance which nobody knows its tone.

I am, yes I am a poem
Which is written in air and water,
Written by thorny hands with ablutions
I am an arrow which is as blunt as the eclipse.

I am the worst in my best and
The best in my worst
I am a chaser of a chased chase,
A reaper of uncultivated corn
And a heart of mixed pitfalls.

I am like a new branch to the tree
Soon to be cut off,
I am like a hook descended in water
I am food which is tasteless to the tasters.
I am a smoldering and raising smoke
I am a poem.

AUTHOR'S NOTES

WHERE I COME FROM
Whether from Burundi, Somalia, South Sudan, Rwanda, Syria, Myanmar...the common answer to this question for a refugee is"CAMP."

RWANDA
The realization that I am from Rwanda gave me inexplicable power. It is a country of a thousand hills. It is also the country of my ancestors.

Nyabarongo: a river in Rwanda
Nyungwe: a National Park in Rwanda
Akagera: a National Park in Rwanda
Sabyinyo: Is a mountain which was volcanic and is between Rwanda and the Democratic Republic of the Congo.

ROAD
There are so many problems in camps, everyone has their own. Mine was an uncertain future.

CRIPPLED MIND
This poem was inspired by a traumatized young man from DRC who I met in Dzaleka Refugee Camp.

LENSES OF MY WISHES
I was the luckiest among my peers, I have both parents...many of my friends, were orphans, from child-headed families or lived with foster families.

SWEET

This poem was inspired by the unspeakable starvation that I noticed whenever I walked around Dzaleka Refugee Camp.

SOUTH AFRICA IS TURNING INTO A GRAVEYARD

This was precipitated by xenophobic torture and brutal killing of 'foreigners' by South Africans, especially in 2019.

CONSOLE MY HEART

This poem was inspired by a Congolese widow whom I met on my way from school. She was carrying a bag and when I offered to help, she said "you remind me of my sons who were killed in a war". I never forgot those words. She was the only remaining from a family of 32 with nails to scratch herself and wait for her box to be sealed.

THE GRAVE OF OUR BEING

At funerals, I always wanted to see the face of the corpse. The reasons for this are completely unknown, but it led me to meditation. This poem was inspired when I saw a corpse of an 11 year-old girl in 2016 in the refugee camp who reportedly died of malnutrition.

DIG HARDER, IT IS DOWN

This poem is a testament to the fact that refugee students were disadvantaged at any school. It is also a testament to their power of survival, resilience and determination.

LIES

Refugees often lie about a better life. This poem is inspired by those lies.

Kinyarwanda: a Rwandan language
Kivu: a lake between Rwanda and DRC

MAMAN AFRICA

This is inspired by "An African Elegy" poem by Ben Okri.

IF DEATH COULD WAIT

In this poem I wanted to explore the responsibility we all have to each other. I created a narrative from the perspective of a person who had died, but wanted to live longer to take care of her children who were homeless and orphans.

AT LEAST SPARE NONE

This poem is inspired by the sad reality that everything in the world is uncertain.

Nyungwe: a national park in Rwanda

PEACE

This poem was inspired by Miriam Dusingize, my classmate in primary and secondary school. She is a girl with whom I have shared beautiful conversations about our shared experiences.

UNHEALED WOUND

This poem was inspired by the traumatized parents that I saw in refugee camps.

LIFE IN A CLOSED CAMP

This poem erupted from the internal debate I had in my head about success.

STEADY MOUNTAIN

This poem was inspired by a Burundian refugee woman who cried inconsolably in front of her husband and her children when she realised that refugee life was unbearable. The sad reality for her was that her life back in Burundi was much better. At least, before her properties were set ablaze. This amplified her mourning and trauma. I was 15 when I heard this story, and I was touched. Then I inked this.

I WAS SOLD

I have always never understood forced marriages or rape. To me, this is beyond murder. This poem was inspired by a short story I read in Form Two; "They sold my sister" by a Kenyan writer Leteipa Ole Sunkuli.

Munyana: Rwandan name for girls, stems from Akanyana which means "a calf"
Urwarwa: a traditional beer made from banana
Inka: a cattle or cow

MINE BELIEF
I realised that the tomorrow of a refugee is determined by the will of well-wishers, from basic amenities like food to the maintenance of their frail hope.

WHEN I CRIED
Hope is the only thing that refugees have wherever they are. Without it, they would remain hopeless forever.

BEFORE I DIE
I made this vow when I learned that I had won a scholarship to Waterford Kamhlaba United World College

DREAMS
Inspired by Maria Manyama, (Tanzania, WK 2020-2021). She asked me what dreams meant to me.

TO WHOM IT MAY CONCERN
Gender-based violence is a constant threat to women in Southern Africa. I wanted to explore this problem by creating a poem from the perspective of a person who experiences rape. I also wanted to touch on how women are not believed: she reports rape to government officials, they deem it is a family issue because she was raped by her step-father.

WHERE I KEPT MY SOUL
This poem is inspired by my hope for a better future. It is inspired by my peers, and other young refugees like me.

YOU ARE MY DESERT

This poem was inspired by a girl I knew who fell pregnant. She was then deserted by her boyfriend, who told her he was not responsible for the pregnancy.

HER

This poem was inspired by one of the conversations I had with Matlala Sefale, Lesotho, a fellow student at Waterford Kamhlaba 2019-2020.

ONLY I

When I realised the power of music, especially African music, I penned this down.

Walahi! Nitasahawu kusali! I swear! I will forget to pray!
Ulembo: beauty
Eeee bwana: Hey man!!
Haki ya Mungu: In the name of God or I swear in the name of God.

COME AND SEE

Inspired by a scene from the camp.

HOLD THOSE KNIVES IN MY HEART

Inspired when I talked to one of the Congolese orphans in Dzaleka refugee camp whose parents had perished in war.

SIT DOWN MY SON

This poem was inspired by one of the stories that my neighbour told. He was an elderly man from the Democratic Republic of the Congo. I would fetch him water from the borehole in exchange for a story.

YOUR DEATH

This poem was inspired by some of the traumatic stories I heard in refugee camps, but it is largely a feat of imagination. I imagined what it would be like for a young girl whose parents have died and she is forced to live with an abusive uncle.

ONLY MY HEART

This poem was inspired by the realization that all my education had been sponsored by people I did not know and wish I knew.

IN THOSE DAYS

A reflection on how far I have come, from walking to Luwani Primary School in Malawi, barefoot to being driven to Waterford Kamhlaba in a school bus.

UNTOLD HEROINE

In refugee camps, there are so many single mothers. I wrote this poem when I realised no one cared or credited their resilience.

FREED FROM HOSTAGE

When I was in IB1 in Waterford Kamhlaba UWCSA, I experienced overwhelming love and kindness from three amazing people: my dear friends, Maru Attwood, Abigail Christ-Rowling and Shivapriya Nair.

UNITED WORLD

I grew up in a community that looked like UWC, so many experiences, so many languages, and so many aspirations. What the real UWC does is add freshness to all those aspirations...that's what I got from UWC, indeed incomparable.

IF I WOULD CREATE

Inspired by the kindness that one friend I knew showed to me.

THANK YOU MOM

When I learned of the resilience of all the mothers in refugee camps...this poem was inspired!

I AM A POEM

I wanted to end the collection with this poem, which is all about hope and excitement. I wrote it when I won a scholarship to attend Waterford Kamhlaba United World College of Southern Africa.

www.ingramcontent.com/pod-product-compliance
Lightning Source LLC
LaVergne TN
LVHW041650060526
838200LV00040B/1780
9780228847120